I0761924

Consider the "Humbler Poet"

—*First of the Series*—

by

Joan Tenner

Consider
the
"Humbler Poet"
—First of the Series—
by
Joan Tenner

Consider the *"Humbler Poet"*

Published by Wisdom House Books, Inc.
Chapel Hill, North Carolina 27517 USA
www.wisdomhousebooks.com

Wisdom House Books is committed to excellence in the publishing industry.

Cover and Interior Design by Ted Ruybal

Published in the United States of America

Hardcover ISBN: 978-1-7332444-6-6
Paperback ISBN: 978-1-7332444-7-3
LCCN: 2023908117

1. POE023000 | POETRY: Subject & Themes - General
2. POE023050 | POETRY: Subject & Themes - Family
3. LCO022010 | LITERARY COLLECTIONS: Subject & Themes General

First Edition 1979 | Second Edition 2018 | Third Edition 2023

25 24 23 22 21 20 / 10 9 8 7 6 5 4 3-

Table of Contents

Joan Tenner

'Humbler Poet'

"WHO is SHE and WHERE has SHE been?"

Joan Tenner was a "woman of her time." Born the year of the great Stock Market Crash (1929), the times, the events and the position of women during the war and after, set the inner fibers of the person she was to become.

Raised during the depression and in a family of seven sibs, one had to be creative with what you had and with three six foot 5+ brothers, with a propensity for practical joking, standing up for oneself became a necessity. So, she grew-up to be spirited, vivacious, energetic and innovative, tackling any problem that got in her way. Yet, as a "woman of her time," Joan was raised and taught, like most women then, that the expected role of a woman was to be the head of a household, a good wife and mother. And that she was!

It was amazing however, that at the end of WWII, it was quickly forgotten how women not only kept their homes operating but kept the factories and mills operating, (a well-established role for men) to support the war effort. After the war, women were sent back to the old established roles of housewife and child bearer. Women had few opportunities or outlets to expand their new-found inner talents and abilities. Women were blocked from typical avenues that were afforded men to rise above this single role. They were often silenced, when topics of politics and other worldly affairs came up. So, efforts to achieve above and beyond their expected roles were difficult.

Joan Tenner however, had one special thing going for her, a talent that evolved at the early age of sixteen. She began to write. Her impressions and thoughts took the form of poetry. Through her writings, a sensitive, intuitive, philosophical and spiritual-self came out. Her poetry became a needed personal extension of herself to the world. Joan's poetry became her voice that expressed her ideas, her opinions, and her impressions and reflections of her world and that of the world beyond her kitchen window as she washed the dishes, cleaned her house and cared for her children.

In this, her first book of poetry, "Consider the "Humbler Poet,"' Joan shares many of her points of view and reflections of a typical enlightened housewife "of her time." The highs and lows; the joys and sorrows of being a woman in the 50's, 60's, 70's, and even today, resonate and can easily be relatable within her work. The gamut of experiences and events that she covers in this book gave it the nickname of "The Mothers' Book." Yet, you will find so much more than the stereotypical housewife and mother as you read.

Inspired *and* Relatable Poetry

Joan Tenner's writings were inspired, early on, by Henry Wadsworth Longfellow who said, "Come read to me some simple heartfelt lay to soothes restless feelings . . . Read from some humbler poet." So, Joan considered her poems as quite ordinary and simple writings; She became the "Humbler Poet!"

I am the "humbler poet"
Humble in words and humble in thought
I pen in a simple way,
Whether ever to be read or not.

Both Longfellow and Joan believed that more people would read more poetry, if they knew they would be able to understand it and not have to waste time trying to figure out what the poet was trying to impart. She believed that most of us would rather know, therefore identify, and relate with the poet's words and expand upon them as they are read, making everyone apart of the poem and even poets themselves.

Who is to say what is pleasing?
Who is to judge what is trite?
The greatest poet on earth might be
A man never taught to write.

Hardly ordinary. Hardly simple. Hardly trite.

The Tenner family hopes that you enjoy this unsung "poet of her time." A wife, a mother, a friend, a poet! Dive into her words, relate and become part of her poems.

We invite you to consider this 'Humbler Poet."

—Mary E. Tenner

2018

From the Author

The collective title of these poems comes from the work of Henry Wadsworth Longfellow. In his poem, "The Day is Done," Longfellow expresses his desire for simplicity. He writes:

"Come, read to me some poem, Some simple and heartfelt lay, That shall soothe this restless feeling, and banish the thoughts of the day."

"Read from some humbler poet"

It has long been my contention that more people would read and enjoy poetry if it were easier to understand. I believe that most of us would prefer not to imagine what the poet is telling us—but to know and therefore be able to identify with it in a positive way. Thus, in all respect, I ask you to:

"Consider the 'Humbler Poet'"

Avocation

Longfellow wrote of the "humbler poet"
Whose "songs gushed from his heart"
Who writes the "simple and heartfelt lay"
To soothe the spirit and peace impart.

I am the "humbler poet,"
Humble in words and humble in thought.
I pen in a simple way,
Whether ever to be read, or not.

Who is to say what is pleasing?
Who is to judge what is trite?
The greatest poet on earth might be
A man never taught to write.

I am the humblest of poets,
If you would but call me so,
Not learned or clever in manner,
But sincere, for this I know.

There is poetry all around us!
All life is a poem, no less.
We must search beyond the obvious
In our quest for happiness.

If I should write one simple poem,
That would soothe one single soul,
Then happy this "humbler poet"
And blessed my humble toil!

The Mood of Morning

Yellow sunlit curtains
Draped the kitchen window pane
And embraced the mood of morning,
Like a gilded picture frame.

A noisy clock kept ticking,
Talking from its mantel perch,
Chiming as the hours went by,
Above the firebrick hearth.

The scent of coffee floated
In the crisp, pure morning air,
While little feet went shuffling
Softly up and down the stair.

Excitement filled each morning.
Every day had its demands,
And so much was accomplished
By these once strong, busy hands.

Gone is the mood of morning
That I felt so long ago.
The house decays in emptiness;
I am feeble now, and slow.

Still, in these quiet moments
That are with me constantly,
I remember the mood of morning,
And the house this used to be.

Ever, Part of the Land

These walls were built
By my grandfather's hand.
He gathered the stones
As he tilled the land.

At each year's planting
The earth would yield
A new crop of stones
To surround his fields.

The stone walls grew
As the seasons passed,
Dividing the fields
From the meadow grass.

Graced by the stones
Gleaned from his land,
The fields took shape,
Formal and grand!

Each stone was lifted
And solidly set.
Each knew his hands
And absorbed his sweat.

Grandfather is gone,
But the stone walls stand.
Thus, he remains
Ever part of this land.

Time Spins

Time flies
On hummingbird wings.

I must do today
The things I must,
Trustfully,
Fulfilling trust.

Time spins
A thinning thread.

I can do today;
It's in my grasp.
Perhaps, today
Will be tomorrow's last.

Time has not
The need of rest.

Urgency commands
What must be done:
Completion of
The many tasks begun.

Time is fading
Just ahead of me.

So little time is left
For me to see
Sufficient
For eternity!

The Natural Way of it

The full of death's great sorrow has not touched me yet,
Except for two new babes for whom life's sun had set
Just as the dawn arrived.
It's true, one lived two days then died.
But I'd not known them yet—not yet.

I can recall my grandmother and dad
Met death when I was only ten. 'Twas sad,
But still, they'd lived a long, long life,
Had raised their young, had borne their strife.
'Twas time for them to rest. 'Twas time.

My mother stood before their open graves,
Controlling tears; for my sake, she was brave.
She said this was "the natural way of it."
"Better child to bury mother, than the opposite."
God spare us both that grief, my Mom and me!

Oh God! Arrange it for us both to be
Beneath the sod, part of eternity,
Before our own are called to make
Death's journey home, to Thee.

Analogy

Happiness grows
Much like a flower.

Duty is the root
Love is the sun
Tears are the rains
Willingness the stem
Toil the bud
Fulfillment the blossom
Happiness the flower.

You might ask "What part
Of the flower is wealth?"
You must answer this
Each for yourself,
In the light of the sun.

The Equalizer

No Whitman, Hawthorne of Keats am I.
However deep the feelings,
Poor the pen.

No beauty of form or face have I.
However great the desire,
Plainest of men.

No scientist, doctor or statesman am I.
Though labored in thought
Slow to progress.

No brave or noble character have I.
However pure the intentions,
Sin and regress

I stumble through a lowly life;
However, minus perfection,
Trust I must.

In His mansions, all will be equal.
However slight I weigh the scale,
God is just.

My Little Prince (or) My Treasure

The soles of babies' feet are soft;
Not yet to walk, are made to kiss.
The tiny toes are fondled oft'
As baby coos to mother's bliss.

My baby smiles and looks around
The nursery, his universe,
Where clowns and animals abound
With silent smiles, their glee converse.

As tiny fingers stretch to reach
The toys around his bed.
His chubby knees go up and down;
He finds his toes instead!

What a priceless gift is he
To guard and daily care for,
To love and guide these little feet,
And say my daily prayers for!

My baby's room becomes a kingdom,
In which he reigns supreme;
My sleepy, hungry little prince
Who smiles from dream to dream.

To Tom, Jr.

Only the best
In life should be
Uppermost
In your memory.

Family picnics
Apple pies
Horseshoe games
Fireflies

Holidays
Christmas joys
Special days
Birthday toys

Easter eggs
Jelly beans
Turkey Day
Halloween

Many houses
Planting trees
Cutting grass
Raking leaves

Picture albums
Souvenirs
Growing up
Parting tears

Homesick heart
Letters home
Renting rooms
On your own

"To Tom, Jr." continues . . .

Lovely girl
Lovely bride
Dad's approval
Mother's pride

All these things
Worthy to be
Uppermost
In your memory.

Best of wishes
All your life.
Worlds of love
For you and wife!

Never question
God's intent
Go His way
And be content

Thank the Lord
For everything
And never stop
Remembering.

Mom

As Written to My Daughter, Carol, 17

Dear Carol,

We talked last night till very late.
We spoke of sex and love and hate,
Discerning what was right and good,
I listened, and I understood.

For, take away the years between,
And I, too, once was seventeen.
I struggled much the same as you,
With doubts and fears and questions, too.

These are special wondrous years,
Decisive and preponderant years.
I understand your deep concern.
Be patient, dear, to live and learn.

I'm grateful for your trust in me
And I admire your honesty.
For your young years of seventeen,
You've shown mature integrity.

I have no cure for all your fears
(Time and life will 'tend to that),
But I am here to dry your tears
(And I thank God for that)!

I haven't much advice to give
On what to do, or how to live:
But know, no matter what you do.
How very much I care for you,
and always will,
Mom

The Death of a Dream

What is, or what may be, is out of my command.
With capacity to accept, but not to understand.
I had hoped and dreamed,
My life to change. Thus rearranged,
Two lives of one is what I'd planned.

With children grown, and on their own,
There is still time and need
To use my talents worthily
Before they turn to seed.
Desperation! Resignation.

Life is cruel, and I'm a fool.
To aim so true, yet not succeed.

The Awakening

I watch as Crocus grow and bloom,
They stand so proud amid their greens!
They are the first to stir and yawn,
The first to wake from winter dreams.

Forsythia follows, bold and golden!
On soft brown branches, dainty wings
Spread the joy of life resuming,
Tickling, taunting sleepy Spring.

Spring stirs and stretches supple limbs
Then takes an April shower.
Fresh and beautiful she'll reign
Over woodland, field and bower.

I watch the Tulips and the Jonquils
Take their place among the proud
Entourage of Spring's surprises
On parade beneath crisp clouds.

I yield to the mood of enchantment
And set all endeavors aside.
Each day for a time, I watch fair Spring
Garnish the countryside.

Coin and Consequence

Life is feather; life is lead.
Feather fluff 'neath anchor, lead.

Life is living, albeit dead.
Living, larruping, with spirit dead.

Hope is clutched, snaps, slips away.
Hope is heaven, dull dreams away.

Love hurts. Life fades. Hearts bleed.
Love's price is life's coin for heart's need.

Hope signs. Death buys a counterfeit coin,
Life's lead. A feather floats. Healed hearts join.

Only love sustained!
Only love remains!

Winter's Euphoria

It's time to store the summer screens
And weather-seal each crack,
To stack the logs, and market hogs,
And bottle apple-jack.

With all the garden goodies jarred,
It's time for pumpkin pie!
With corn shocks stacked, potatoes sacked,
We'll watch the snow geese fly.

The roof is fixed and feather ticks
Are taken out of storage.
Our breakfast fare will soon be changed
To coffee and hot porridge.

A hoarfrost came this morning
To bestow its kiss of death,
Precursor of the winter-tide,
With silent icy breath.

I love the coming wintertime
With all its peaceful charm,
Bringing quiet benediction
Unto our little farm.

Devoid of all the trials and toil
That other seasons bring,
We'll live in thankful retrospect
Until once more, its spring.

The Magic Scent of Pine

A small, ungainly Christmas pine
Stood in a corner space
Of a large and dreary hall
In a lonely drafty place.

Wrapped in quiet, bleak and still,
No sparkling lights to trim the tree,
No flaming logs to chase the chill
Nor cheer replace monotony.

This shelter for abandoned aged,
A purgatory more than less,
Is quiet while a gay world frolics
Drenched in Yuletide happiness.

Though Holy Eve, no one has left
The room of his existence.
I longed to hear a Carol sung
And sounds of "Merry Christmas."

Quite suddenly, from out the night
A magic vapor, scent of pine,
Crept into my consciousness
And touched this soul of mine.

Sweet melodies of memories
Of Christmases gone by
Emerged from out my quickening heart
Like fountains toward the sky!

Such sudden change came over me!
As Christmas love did penetrate
My anxious spirit did embrace
And gave it cause to celebrate.

"The Magic Scent of Pine" continues . . .

I took deep breaths there near the tree.
The scent of pine grew stronger still.
It seemed a miracle had brought
A sense of joy beyond my will!

And while I stood, etherealized,
A shuffling sound made me aware.
A fragile figure stood nearby
With lowered eyes as if in prayer.

He spoke, with breathy, cracking voice.
"How shines the Christmas Star tonight?"
"I haven't felt its glow for years;
It seems to me no longer bright.

Then fell a ghastly silence!
My heart heaved and heavy ached.
How could the joy I felt be shared
With this poor man, so desolate?

I said "Dear Sir, the Christmas Star
Is sacrosanct, will always shine!
You must believe it shines tonight!
Come, share a secret that is mine."

"Touch this little Christmas tree.
Breathe deep and smell the pine.
Let the magic of its scent
Permeate your soul and mind!"

He hesitated, then complied,
His rugate face without expression.
I prayed "Oh come Emanuel!
Lift his spirit from depression.

"The Magic Scent of Pine" continues . . .

The Christmas Star, as in tradition,
Truly graced our world that night,
And as it was of long ago,
Again, became a guiding light.

We each received a gift to share
Of friendship warmly felt.
There was no finer gift exchanged
In all this world of wealth.

For all you aged, now abandoned
By the world you helped project,
Rid your hearts of bitterness,
Forgive your progenies' neglect!

There is a greater love to tend you
And His star will ever shine!
We can feel his omnipresence
In the magic scent of pine!

To Claudine

Your world is made of feathers,
Always fluttering with the breeze!
You must strain to keep them fettered,
Lest fidget fate decide to sneeze!
Lest troubled winds beset them soaring
Out of reach then out of sight,
Lest season's storm should come a roaring,
Make a fist and hold them tight!

How much do your feathers weigh?
How many do they count?
As years do mark the passing days
So do your feathers mount.
At times they seem a heavy weight
Grasping thus, in dread and fear,
Clutching, keeping them from flight,
Holding tight another year.

Know one day your world of feathers
Will escape and scatter far.
Joys of love and sound and sight
Will cease, such as they are,
Will waft away beyond your grasp
And, one by one, go sailing
Through misty fog of in between
The winning and the failing.

Of count and weight be not concerned.
Allotments have been preordained.
For each and every child of man,

"To Claudine" continues . . .

The feather count is prearranged.
Hold fast each one as Godly given,
Satisfied to know not when
The will of heaven will disperse them,
Never to be clutched again.

Tribute

Today, a golden acorn fell
From the royal oak of life.
As mortal life did terminate,
This precious seed did germinate,
And Immortality emerged,
Amid angelic chorus, surged
Into the aura of forever.

The tree of life, this royal oak,
Has countless acorns in its boughs.
Not all are golden, just a few.
You were golden, through and through,
The most radiant fruit that a tree could bear!
A privilege mine, your bough to share.
I shall miss the gleam of your mettle.

Inevitably

Age, and the wisdom to accept it,
Comes to each of us
Slowly, but inevitably.

Humility creeps upon the soul,
As the rays of the setting sun,
Slowly, but inevitably.

Youth's beauty and self-assurance
Fade, like the bloom of the lily,
Slowly, but inevitably.

The Maker brings us to Himself,
And sifts the clay that housed the soul,
Slowly, but inevitably.

The Me I Want to Be

"To be understood" how very unique!
Were I my own sincere critique,
I would not know me better than any other!

So much of me is not quite clear
To even me, though I am nearer
To the secrets of my soul, than any other.

Sometimes I think if I spoke out clearly,
To myself, so that I could hear me,
I would find me to be different than any other.

But alas! Sometimes, the words that pass my lips
Have taste as vile as poison sips;
A weakness of mine, more than any other.

In a pseudo web of conceit, I am caught,
Wanting to know me as I am not,
With kindness and virtue, more than any other.

So thus it is clear, I must constantly try to
Understand me, and eternally strive to
Be the me I want me to be, more than any other!

In Despair

I must find one good reason to live!
I'm drowning in despair and disappointment.

Even my dreams are no more.
Hope is gone. I care not for love.
Each day is a duty, nothing more.
I look out to the world for some reason
And find none.
There are those who bear horrendous ills,
Yet they care more for life than I.
Death is invited, longed for,
Dared and coaxed to come for me.

I am level with the ground,
But I lay six feet above my goal.
Life has lost its challenge, its allure.
I have done nothing worth doing
But I've spent a lifetime of toil.
Hard work and accomplishment then,
Seem stupid and futile now.
Love is dead, and I am cold to life.
I cannot hate, but cannot understand
How love, so deep could so evaporate.

All will to dust return, eventually.
Why not sooner? End this farce!
Stop the eternal budding of the trees,
Flowing of the earth,
And replenishing the herd!
At least make it stop for me.
Give me rest and relief.
Silence my grief!
I am a walking sepulcher.
How can one love without reason?

"In Despair" continues . . .

by Joan Tenner

Still, in all my deep despair, I cannot defy Him
Who commands me to breathe and to live.
If, after this, a life exists
I must have a better one.
An eternity of unhappiness, inescapable,
Is all that prevents a razor to my wrists.
So, in my search for one reason to live,
I have discovered it in a promise I once read.
"Ask and you shall receive, that your joy may be full."
And so, I shall ask, shall plead, shall beg, and
Find peace.

Worlds in Words

The sea is a world of mystery.
Massive and powerful, awesome,
Dark on darker to deeper and deeper
Abyss, gravity sucking all things
Under, asunder, down and down
To the bottomless bottom of imagination,
Supposition and dread!

The wind is indefatigable.
The incubus of the mountain top,
Bitter, whipping, moaning
Resentment to the intruder.
Jealous, that anyone could climb
So high, to hear him thrash against
The gigantic mountain side.
Relentless, merciless,
Force against might,
Against the rock and the granite,
Making slow progress
In scarring the world,
But never resting not admitting
The desire to be still
And to rest a while,
To contemplate the beauty of its victim!

The pen is equally great and unique.
Indigo spread on the parchments of time,
Recording life and death,
Accounting for coin and consequence,
Registering man's thoughts
And God's laws.

"Worlds in Words" continues . . .

by Joan Tenner

Each author an individualist,
Yet all of certain worth and weight!
Each relentless,
By day and by night,
Creating worlds in words.
Some to be treasured as classics,
Others yet destined
Never to be read at all.
Hurry! Hurry! Write it down,
Lest your thoughts be lost forever!

In Anger

Liar! False in jumbled tracks!
Wander 'round a widening pit!
Skirt the issues—bend the facts,
Twist the truth to falsely fit!

Lost in a maze of the lies you told,
Respect will skip beyond your reach;
The credence of your words dissolve
Like friendships, that your lies did breach.

Image true 'til mirror cracks,
Liar false to self and all,
Unless with truth your lies retract,
Woe to you at judgment call!

A word so vile defiles my pen!
Liar! Imitating Eden's snake!
I shall not write of it again,
And must forgive for heaven's sake

Truth

It is the waking from a dream,
The only peace in conflict,
The aqua vitae of the soul,
The issue of the prophets.

In the war between concepts
Of right versus wrong,
The undaunted victor
Immortally strong.

A force ever striving
Since the serpent, to Eve,
Created the lie,
With intent to deceive.

Lone weapon of Justice,
Blind to consequence,
A tenacious defender
Of pure innocence.

Truth is the perfection of thought,
The sole essence of Utopia,
The scourge of the immoral,
The final judgement of God.

Sunrise on Padre Island

From the strand on Padre Island
To the limits of the sea
And beyond the far horizon
I would view God's artistry.

Anxiously, I watched the skies,
Looking East to see the sun
Overtake and chase the darkness
From the day that had begun.

In the scant, dim light of dawning,
Imaginative and aware,
I saw so much of interest
That I never dreamed was there!

Two dragons sprang up from the sea,
Monsters, standing back to back,
And formed in close proximity
Two great, dense clouds in shades of black.

The dragons turned and intertwined
Locked in battle for a time,
'Til loosing shape and density,
Dispersed into infinity!

Then, Sea Gulls came in sudden flight
From no-where, and with graceful motion,
Soared into the dawn, then swooped
To kiss their image on the ocean.

The sky resembled mother-of-pearl
Soft pink and blue on oyster white.
The sea, a pane of glass became,
Shimmering in reflected light.

"Sunrise on Padre Island" continues . . .

by Joan Tenner

The sun, afire, broke into view,
With awe inspiring majesty!
The then changed to deeper blue.
The earth spun "round in ecstasy'!

How restful is the dark of night.
How inspirational, the dawn!
How insignificant I seem,
Compared to this phenomenon!

Who?

Could the man in the moon be a woman,
With myriad stars in her gown?
Could the moon glow be her golden hair
Adorned with a star-studded crown?

Could the Milky Way be a flowing cape,
Made of finest velvet and lace?
Could the Seven Little Sisters be jesters
Who keep that smile on her face?

Could the planets all be jewels
With gleaming facets, sparkling bright?
A necklace flawless and unique
Twinkling, twinkling in the night.

Could the Dipper be her scepter,
A symbol of her powers,
As she rules with splendid majesty,
The soft night's darkest hours?

How often do I wonder
At this great reflected stature!
If she is mirrored from the earth,
Could she be mother nature?

(This was written at age 16, in 1945 when space was still an enchanting world of whatever one's imagination might make it.)

Perspective

Looking down
Through the window of a plane in flight,
I marvel
At the beauty of the cities at night!

They sparkle!
Like diamond-dust on a coal-black bed,
A mirror
Of the view of the stars overhead.

Looking down
Like a god from his universe,
Not humbly
As from earth, the view in reverse.

How changed
My perspective, with my point of view!
Heretofore,
Viewing earth was for gods to do.

Search in the Glass

I'm staring in the mirror, eye to glass,
And searching deep within my dimming eyes.
I see just me. It can't be me!
But me I can't disguise.

I'm staring in the mirror, eye to glass.
I'm frightened of the dim uncertain gray!
Perhaps I'll find the something I can blame.
Some evil, rotting, taking sight away.

"What demon dims my eyes?" I ask!
"What devil drowns to deeper dark
The light I need to see the world
To give my due, to make my mark?"

It can't be me! I would not do
This awful thing! It must be someone else.
It can't be me, but me I see;
Yet deeper search, search deeper, self!

There is someone!! In glassy black,
Look! Staring back at me!
Deep down behind the small black hole,
Look closer, strain to see!

This evil thing, elusive in the glass,
Is hiding from my stare, deep, deep inside.
Perhaps it's me! It must be me,
Obtuse and hard to recognize.

How long has evil lived with me?
Each man has secret sin.
The good parades without disguise,
But evil hides within.

"Search in the Glass" continues . . .

The search is done! I leave the glass.
I've found someone to blame.
The culprit hides within myself
And Evil is his name.

When darkness comes, and I can't see
The glass that mirrors me,
Then Evil be as Evil does!
He won't look back at me.

(Also, could be entitled "On the Edge of Blindness")

To Console

A part of their father
A part of me
A part of God
Eternally.

Two of our babes
Beneath the sod
Are truly safe
In the arms of God.

One Small Request

To die, content to die, seems
Such a simple, small request
Of one Who sits the cosmic clocks
And puts the day to rest.

Let me live to see the morning
Once more overcome the night.
To breathe my last of morning air
Before my soul takes flight.

Smiling, will I then succumb
Unto the tomb that open waits,
Grateful for my granted wish
I will this tender time embrace.

To die, content to die, is all I ask.
Pray let it be.
Fix the dazzling view of morning
On my eyes eternally.

Send my spirit forth in sunlight
As it separates from me,
To probe that promised afterlife
Of timeless mystery.

Think Again!

What author pens a book,
Then burns it ere it can be bound?
What farmer plows and plants,
Then plucks the seedling from the ground?
Strange indeed, behavior such! Unnatural

Beware! Lest stifled souls of babes unborn
Unite to right the wrong so casually done;
And armed with hate,
Should seek the aid of angels,
Guardians robbed of duties just begun.
Strange indeed, such thoughts as this! Unnatural.

What a vengeful army
Would that alliance make!
God help the souls of men
Who cannot sense the sin!
Quiescent conscience of the world,
You must thing again.
It makes no sense to write then burn,
To plant then pluck,
Nor kill what we begin.
Strange indeed, behavior such! Unnatural!

The Judgement

Once, a trial was held
To weigh the worth
Of two immortal souls.

The two spirits were
Disguised as men:
One in black,
Like the silt of the ocean floor,
And one in white,
Like the arid sands of the desert.

The trial was long,
Tense and tiring,
But the Judge
Was perceptive and just.

After the trial was over,
Divine waters washed away
Their disguises.
The Judge uplifted the souls,
One in each of His hands,
And proclaimed them
Each "alike."

With equal mercy and tenderness,
Perpetual light shown upon them,
And they rested, in peace.

Evaluation

I see such things of shape and hue
That be within my scope and view.
I cannot see beyond the hour,
Possessing no prophetic power,
No expectations or illusions.
No false fancies or delusions,
Still, I have faith.

The things that happen, day by day,
All work to good in some strange way.
The past cannot be rearranged.
Fact and deed cannot be changed.
Though sorrow cause my heart to swell,
To pound, to beat at the brink of hell,
Still, I have hope.

To property I state no claim,
Nor pedigree, or chance of fame.
No matter, for there is no need,
When all the earth's my family,
When there are millions just like me.
Made of clay and soul are we.
So, I have love.

Thus, what I see or think or say
May not exist beyond today,
But I have shared the gifts of earth,
Possess a soul, was given birth!
It is enough that I am me,
And heir to all eternity!
There's nothing else.

Perhaps Next Monday

Once a year, I like to clean
And paint, and fix things right.
These chores are called "spring cleaning."
It's every housewife's plight.

In spring, I get spring fever.
Summer's heat must let work wait.
When fall comes, its too beautiful!
By winter, it's too late.

And so, the months fly by for me,
Procrastinate, defer, delay.
I know the house is going to pot
A little more each day.

But I enjoy the kids, the dog,
And family fun and games,
And playing bridge and eating out,
And TV when it rains.

This big old house is warm and kind,
And will wait until that someday,
When I'll decide "it's cleaning time."
Perhaps I'll start next Monday.

Of Wealth And Worth

Sift out your wealth like golden nuggets
From a clump of clay.
Sort out the worth and refine it from
The ore of yesterday,

Our lives should be like a smelting pot
Of effort and pain,
Made pure by the fire of intentions,
And forged into gain.

Brilliant jewels should be set within
The tempered gold of life,
Jewels of grand and worthy deeds
As recompense for strife.

Gather a fortune of this kind of wealth
Such as you cannot hold.
It cannot be bought or stolen from you
Not traded or sold.

It's a special kind of wealth that makes
Life worth the living.
The only gain that is tax exempt while
You get from giving.

It's a rare opulence that benefits all
And compounds with age,
The only wealth with purchasing power
That transcends the grave.

You can't judge a man who lacks possessions
And monetary worth,
For he may well be, through his charity,
The richest man on earth!

Take Courage

Flaunt your colors!
There is time for beauty, still.

In the Autumn woods
here is no fear of death!
The trees have courage
To show beauty in demise.
There is no fear
Beneath their chaste disguise.
Taking cover 'neath a pall
Of color, bold and vivid,
Though waning, still intrepid!
Which tree has beauty most?
Compare each to the other.
Neither shames the other,
Yet, each is unsurpassed!
Who fixed the patterns?
Who mixed the shades?
Such beauty is undreamable,
Beyond imagination!
Yet, it is real, yet lives
In splendor, gives
Its spirit to a wintry death,
Awaiting Spring's
Resurrective breath,
To live again the cycle.

The Voice of Our God

Hear the powerful sounds of the sea!
Percussions of water, wave after wave,
Striking the shore in manner grave,
Much like a sinner striking his breast
Invoking the Lord for mercy in rest.

With the roar of a monster, it stretches tall,
Humps and curls in caterpillar fashion,
Then lunges, dropping with cataclysmic action.
Downward it plunges to the depth of the sea,
Acting, reacting, incessantly.

Hear the whipping sound of the wind!
Cyclop's kin, with penetrating force,
Blasting, bemoaning in threatening voice,
Scarring the land, molesting the sea,
In a boastful show of hostility.

Consider the sound of the writer's pen,
Scratching and scrawling torrents of ink,
To amuse, to record, to make man think,
Expounding, exhorting, to enrich and impart
Knowledge to the mind, emotion to the heart.

Listen! These sounds are not without message!
They are engendered traits of the earth,
God driven energies of infinite worth.
The voice of our God can be heard within
The sound of the sea, the wind and the pen.

"How can this be?" You may question me.
"Sea sounds are harsh and indignatious;
Wind sounds are rough and affrontatious;

"The Voice of Our God" continues . . .

The scratch of the pen is hardly sublime.
And the fruit of man's mind is far from divine!"

Still, these notable sounds that echo 'round
Seem sure to me, God's voice to be,
Scolding, and warning humanity.
"When will you do as I asked of thee?"
"My greatest commandment is Charity!"

Think, as you listen to wind and sea!
From eons of time to the conscience of men
They have challenged thought and inspired the pen.
Though the kingdom, power and glory are Thine,
The dutiful sound of Thy pen is mine.

To Ponder

A patriotic and noble son,
At the call of his government,
Avowed to bravely do his part,
And, unquestioning, he went.

She spoke, hurry-scurry of trivial things,
As her son left home to the war.
She desperately tried to conceal the fear
That she would see him no more.

He smiled, then said, "Don't worry."
She nodded, "Be sure to write."
Then, for a moment, their silence spoke
All the things that were right.

With quivering lips, a hasty kiss,
And he was gone. She heaved "that sigh"
Of all other mothers of other sons
Who had said that same "goodbye."

Recalling the labor-pains of his birth
And the years since he left her womb,
She wondered if destiny had contrived
All this, for a soldier's tomb.

It has been so, in all generations.
War's river of blood runs deep!
It ripples with torrents of tear drops,
While unquestioning, they sleep.

The world is ever at war somewhere,
And always mothers weep.
War's river of blood runs over!
Yet, unquestioning, they sleep.

My 'Sponsibility

Strawberries, strawberries
How are you today?
I'm just fine and dandy
Would you like to play?

I'm going to play "farmer"
And pick all that are red!
My daddy says "it's time
You were leaving your bed!"

I hoed you this spring
And watered you plenty.
I counted your blossoms
All 'hundred and twenty!

Next year there'll be more
Pretty berries for me,
And that's a good thing
'cause there'll be more of me!

My daddy says I'll grow a lot
And then, when I am six
I'll have to start to go to school
To learn some 'rithmetic.

Now, which of you would like to be
The very first one tasted?
You'll all be sure to have your turn
'cause not one will be wasted!

Oh! Here is a fat one!
But you are still green.
I like only red ones
To swim in my cream!

"My 'sponsibility" continues . . .

Here's one for Daddy
And two for my Gramps
And one for my Mommy
And two for my Aunts.

And here's the one for me!
It's the biggest I see!
Oh! It's fun to play farmer
And pick sweet strawberries!

I'd better take you in the house.
My hands are much too small.
I wouldn't want to squeeze you,
You'd be no good at all!

I'll come again tomorrow
And every day I can.
I'm going to eat strawberries
'til I'm a grown-up man!

My daddy says that everyone
Should grow a plant or two,
To learn 'sponsibility.
I'm 'sponsible for you!

And gee, I'm glad I hoed you
And watered you and all!
I'm awful glad I growed you,
It wasn't hard at all.

I learned more than 'sponsibility.
I learned some 'rithmetic.
I counted 'hundred and twenty!
And I'm not even six!

"My 'sponsibility" continues . . .

My daddy says he's proud of me,
And I am proud of you.
My daddy's 'sponsible for me.
I'm 'sponsible for you!

Strawberries, sweet berries,
It's been such fun to know you!
I'm glad you'll come again next Spring
So, I can help to grow you.

Caught!

I saw you sneak that second piece of cake!
In the future, please be quiet
And don't speak to me of diet,
When your shirts no longer button at the waist!

You think that I don't notice how you cheat!
I am tired of all your chatter
Of how you diet and grow fatter
It's quite obvious that you "are" what you eat.

I recall you took up jogging late last year.
You went out running every day,
But stopped for snacks along the way,
Then, came riding home with friends, to have a beer.

You'll have to count your calories on your own.
Your figure's out of kelter
But you're giving "me" to ulcer!
The pounds you want to shed must be your own!

So Heaven Can Be

I lay to rest with a shattered heart.
It will not mend by the 'morrow.
The break too complete, the pain too great,
How can I live with such sorrow?

Our hearts were welded together,
He gave me purpose for each day.
He was my joy, my aorta, my life.
He's gone. I've lost him and my way.

I know he's suspended in Limbo
Searching and waiting for me.
Somehow, we must be together
Again, joined in eternity.

Come, grim Reaper, gleam your field!
With one swift swing of your scythe,
Waft me over the Sea of Styx
To descend at my lover's side.

Eternal peace cannot be ours
Until we are together.
Only then can heaven be,
And after that—forever.

Sequel – So Heaven Can Be

Somehow, I slept in my sepulcher of sorrow.
Regretfully, I woke, my prayer unfulfilled.
The Reaper had not gleaned his field
Not swung his scythe as I had willed.

From my window I could see the world
Bustling, as though nothing has changed.
All living things were performing
As nature had so prearranged.

The sun hung in its usual place
As it has for eons of time.
The heart of the universe was whole
And oblivious to mine.

So, I must exist with half a heart,
And half a soul as well,
With the other half in Limbo
Beyond the reach of hell.

Time, on earth, will go its course
And time in heaven spin,
But time in Limbo must be still
Until I come to him.

Meanwhile, I must serve the time
That fate had me intended;
Stay within the Reapers plan,
"Til life for me is ended.

I must believe he's waiting
Where time will timeless be.

"Sequel – So Heaven Can Be" continues . . .

One day, I shall join my love
Then come—infinity!

Eternal peace cannot be ours
Until we are together.
Only then can heaven be,
And after that—forever!

At the Kitchen Sink

When all of my children were small and at home,
I had hardly a moment to call my own.
I neglected the things that I used to do
And the problems increased as the family grew!

Efficiency was the 'goal' for each day,
So I 'taught" myself to efficiently pray.
I chose all the small chores
That seemed so depressing
And I did each one,
Giving thanks for a blessing.

At the sink in the kitchen,
As I washed each dish,
I spoke to the Lord
Of each need, each wish.
As I straightened each bed,
I would say a small prayer
That God would protect
The child who slept there.

While making the bed
For my husband and me,
I would pray for his safety, and gradually,
The chores of the morning
Were admirably done,
Without having resented a single one.

Our family was blest.
The children are grown.

"At the Kitchen Sink" continues . . .

by Joan Tenner

There is little to do.
My time is my own.
I write poems and read;
I sew, and I think;
But I still say my prayers
At the kitchen sink.

A Caution

Do not force anyone
An absurdity to defend.
Rather, ignore it
And retain a friend.
Otherwise, embarrassed,
Himself, will despise
And you will be held
With contempt in his eyes.

Neither take offense
From statements rash
When vexation transforms
Tongue into lash.
Rather, be patient
And calmly reply.
Say nothing harsh
Not his anger defy.

Strive for self-control.
Peace is worth the cost.
There is no calamity
Like a friendship lost.

by Joan Tenner

The Agreement

For years they had known
hey'd marry when grown.
To be never alone
Was their plan

Yards of white lace,
A radiant face,
Her finger graced
By his ring.

Wine glasses, cake dishes,
Friends and good wishes,
Bon voyage kisses,
At the reception.

Alone in their room,
A virgin and groom
On a honeymoon
Of disappointment.

No consummation;
With no explanation,
Only frustration
Did ensue.

Suppressing their need,
Each one agreed
Not to be freed
From their vows.

They shared instead
A platonic bed
As pure as the thread
Of their love.

"The Agreement" continues . . .

Never regretful
And ever grateful,
Both were faithful
To each other.

Then, old and unstable,
One was disabled,
The other unable
To care for both.

Quite willing, they died
In contrived suicide,
Still side by side
And forever.

Can we condemn
Either of them
For such a sin?
I think not.

by Joan Tenner

First Stop, Earth?

Today, I'm here on planet Earth.
Who knows how long I'll stay?
How and where I go from here
I really cannot say.

I, like every other man,
Give quite a bit of thought
To my belief in afterlife,
If it exists or not.

Is Earth our point of origin,
And final destination?
Or is it so, as I believe,
That death means transformation?

If my soul should go to sleep
Along with me, to never waken,
Then, I suppose I end with me,
And my credos are mistaken.

I believe there is a God.
It is His Earth and He knows best.
He gave me my immortal soul
Restrained, contained in bone and flesh.

I have no proof, but I have faith.
Examine well a single rose;
Observe a child; watch a sunrise.
By this, a man learns what he knows.

Concept of Paradise

Locked in grief, as grief
Does paralyze the breast
And make it labor so
To draw each breath,
My being strains to self-contain
The bitter burden lest
It spill and drown
Earth's gentle joys of birth.

Locked in grief and hope
That this interlude be brief
When my heart is separate
From his, now discarnate.
Our ties, too strong
To be by death dissolved,
So great was our resolve
To be forever one.

Locked in grief, until
With mortal shells dispersed,
Like atoms, magnetized,
Our souls will fuse and form
A particle of paradise,
An element of grace
To orbit 'round the Deity
Who blessed our joyful joining.

I Thought I Loved You Then

I met thirty years ago
And thought I loved you then.

I thought I loved you completely
When our love was pure enchantment.
I only thought I loved you
When we married, long ago.
Yet, as the years went by,
My love for you did grow
To such dimensions
Until the love I feel today
Is so remote, in many ways,
From the love I felt when
I thought I loved you, then.

You taught me to express love
Without reservation.
To say "I'm sorry" sincerely,
Without hesitation.
You forgave, when in anger
Harsh things I said,
Never returning hurt for hurt
But kindness instead.
You made me aware of the dignity
And the plight of the needy.
You taught me to share my life
And to pity the greedy.

If there is anything remarkable
In me or our children,
It came from your example.
You never compromised

"I Thought I Loved You Then" continues . . .

Your sense of fairness and right.
To the cause of convenience or gain.

Though your language, at times,
Can be coarse and rough,
You are more "Christian'
Than anyone I've known.
Never acting ostentatiously,
You quietly do the charitable deed.

You have bound your heart to mine
In quiet chains.
The links formed strong between us
One by one,
Each time there was a need fulfilled
One for the other.
You have been tender, supportive,
And ever understanding.
You have made me happy
And content to be a part of you.
I no longer function as me.
I am we.

I met you thirty years ago
And thought I loved you then;
But there is love, and there is love.
With constant aboundings,
Its essence has reached to infinity
From whence it returns an echo
Forever resounding in my heart.

Art Par Excellence

Art, par excellence,
Is on parade,
In the gallery colossus
Of the forest glade!

See spectacular landscapes!
Enjoy the revue
Of exceptional colors
'Neath a ceiling of blue!

There's music provided
By the Autumn breeze,
The birds' sweet songs
And the rustling leaves.

Kowtow to King Oak
And bow to the pine,
For structure and color
Majestically fine!

In contrast and highlight,
The aspen excel!
The birch and the maple
Do almost as well.

Each species of tree,
Each curve of the land,
Is accountable to
The Artist's firm hand.

Notice the detail
Of each creation;
The pinecones, acorn,
And leaf crenation's.

"Art Par Excellence" continues . . .

The catkin and berries,
And vines intertwined,
Seed pods and weed rods,
Precisely designed.

Applause! To the Artist,
The Master Hand,
Who created this scene,
So skillfully planned.

Don't miss the art show
Now on parade,
In the gallery colossus
Of the forest glade!

The Message

The auto shrieked and skidded!
That horrid sound is with me yet.
I saw him hit and thrown into
The mangled corpse I can't forget.

I rushed to hold my little boy,
To kiss and comfort him.
He made no sound. His startled eyes
Looked into mine, then closed again.

I pressed my ear against his heart.
It stopped. Mine did the same.
I died a sort of living death;
In agony, I screamed his name!

Time became an empty chasm,
As I kissed his little hands and head.
Then, someone tapped my shoulder softly,
"Please, let him go. Your boy is dead."

Smothering shadow seized my mind.
I shook him, but he did not waken.
I laid him down reluctantly,
Hope and disbelief, forsaken.

Confused, I prayed for understanding.
I prayed that God would show me "why"
With so many ill and aged,
Why a little child should die!

No answer came to comfort me.
Though friends had offered sympathy,
I listened only passively.
My fragile faith was failing me!

"The Message" continues . . .

Then I recalled a dear old friend
Who, when by grief or doubt perplexed,
Would find a message in the Bible
In a random chosen text.

I took the Bible from the shelf
And drew it open, hurriedly!
With my finger, I selected
Hopefully, God's words to me.

I read: Suffer the little children
To come unto me." Thankfully,
I sobbed, "Forgive me Lord!"
"I know he's safe with Thee."

Forever "Why"

After the earth quakes,
After the sea breaks
Over the strand,
After the mountains shake,
Settle and form take
The shape of new lands,
After the tremors calm,
The bodies embalmed
And funerals done,
After the rituals of sorrow
Fade, after tomorrow,
A new world is begun.

Temperamental Earth
Twists Death and Birth
Around each other;
In forced embrace,
Face to face
They enfold each other,
Exchange one breath,
To Life from Death
With futile resistance.
For a moment, stay they,
Then break away, each
To a new existence.

Why does Dame Earth
Sanction rebirth
And support it,
Then twist and wallow,
Open and swallow
They, abort it?

"Forever 'Why'" continues . . .

Pregnant with life,

Instigating death,
Both cradle and pyre,
Why does she heave,
And so violently
Spew lava and fire?

Those who lie still
Entombed deep in the rills
Of crumpled hills,
Lament and moan,
In sibilant tones
As dry as their bones
Ad infinitum sigh,
Evoking reply,
Ever questioning "Why?"

Eons ensue and pass.
Still, the meadow grass
Greens in Spring.
Though inside-out,
Earth dances about
Her orbital ring,
Accompanied by
An eddy of sighs
Ever whispering "Why?

Who Will Teach

Liberated woman, what have you done?
Avoided your daughter, ignored your son.
How can you mold them
Without patient correction?
How can you guard them
Without constant protection?
How can you leave them
So soon after birth?
Who will convince them
Of your love and their worth.

You have forfeited your place
In the family
Liberated, yes,
But still not free.
You have traded the best
Of a natural life,
For a woman's need
Is to be a wife.
Liberated woman, of what are you free?
From all that you're meant for naturally.

Your children are incorrigible!
What did you expect?
Their conduct deplorable
Because of your neglect.
Children must be taught
What is wrong and what is right,
And be tenderly tucked
Into bed at night.
They need to learn kindness
And how to forgive.

"Who will Teach Continues" continues . . .

Who will teach them to pray
And how not to live.

If you are a mother
You have made your decision.
Dedicate yourself
To your commission.
There'll be lots of time.
After they've grown,
But first, be a mother,
They need you at home.

Poet or Fool?

Am I poet or fool?
I see this real as abstract,
Describing not the fact
But the abstract as real,
In what I see and what I feel.

Am I poet or fool?
And is there a difference?
With kindly indifference
A fool is tolerated,
Neither loved not hated.

If I be poet then why
Are my words ineffective,
Ignored as misdirected,
Unheard as though unspoken,
Mute as silence, unbroken?

Perhaps I am a fool
And unworthy of attention,
Too trite to even mention—
The whole of my endeavor
Too remote, too unclever.

Am I poet or fool?
Perhaps I am each.
Perhaps I write to reach
The hearts of other fools like me.
Who can judge with certainty?

How Poor I Would Be . . .

Every so often, when I was a child,
We would visit my grandfather's farm.
I remember the rutted, rock-cluttered road
That led to a clearing, down by the barn.

Field-stones were set in a series of wall
That blocked-in the wheat and the corn.
An orchard of fruit on the high-ground.
Graced the farm house where mother was born.

In the family Ford, (which was technically
The finest car made in the industry)
We each took our places, obligingly
And all of us fit, miraculously!

The car trunk was packed and tied to a rack
Perched on the back of the car.
The tires were checked, the doors all locked,
And the windows left slightly ajar.

The dad would say, "Mother, are you very sure
That you've packed all you planned to take?"
A turn of the crank, (out in front of the car)
And the motor complied with a sputter and a shake.

All seven children, my mother and dad,
Were delighted to be on our way!
It seemed that we drove for hours.
Forty miles was such a long way!

The last turn-in was grandfather's road
It was shady, winding and bumpy in spots.
We know we were close to the farm (for sure)
When we bounced and jostled over the rocks

"How Poor I Would Be" continues . . .

by Joan Tenner

When grandfather saw our car on his road,
He would open the swinging gate,
And we'd drive right into the barn-yard
Where my grandmother would wait.

After the hugs and the greetings,
We quickly unloaded the car.
Then, we feasted on grandmother's cookies,
Always kept in an earthen jar.

Grandfather would show us the new calves and shoats,
And we'd throw corn cobs to the hogs.
We'd give the horses a hand full of oats.
And would try to make friends with the dogs.

We children ate dinner outside, on the steps
That led to the winter-house door,
While the grown-ups ate in the summer house
Where they chatted for hours and more.

Today, as I look at old photographs
And recall those wonderful years,
It seems that my memory sharpens
And the time-span between disappears.

Grandfather was tall, wore coveralls,
And spoke German, his native tongue.
He and grandmother came to this land
When newly married and very young.

Their children were born and raised on this farm,
And, we as grandchildren, fortunately,
Could come to enjoy what they had achieved
Through love, labor and constancy.

"How Poor I Would Be" continues . . .

With few restrictions, we'd spend these days In the way each child liked the best.
There were spiders to watch, and houseflies to swat
And butterflies to catch.

There were crawdads to fetch from the mountain stream, There was time to jump in the hay.
There were berries to pick, and chickens to chase,
And nothing to do but play!

We'd take off our shoes and wiggle our toes
In the icy-cold watering trough.
We'd visit the kittens and cats in the barn,
And play Tarzan from high in the loft.

Soon evening would come. The milking was done
And we'd know it was time for Good-byes.
Even my mom was reluctant to leave.
I could tell by the tears in her eyes.

Such were the days, ever part of my heart!
I still tell my children about them.
Such were the treasures my parents gave me.
How poor I would be without them.

June 2, 1977

He has taken the high road! He can look back and see
His wife and children bid him fond farewell.

He has taken the high road. Just up ahead he sees The
light, where forever he will dwell.

The traveling is easy now. He has no burdens.
His legs no longer ache, nor does he tire along the way,

He has taken the high road. Our love goes with him.
Our hearts are forever entwined. Let us pray.
"Give to him eternal rest, and in time, grant us the same
Comfort us who miss him. This, we ask in Jesus' name."

Sight to Remember

One pleasant Autumn afternoon,
On a lake of brilliant blue,
Through fluffy white duck feathers
A soft wind blew,
Rippling the waters that bore my canoe.

I did not row once I had reached
The middle of the lake.
At ease, I watched the sky drift by
Beneath a drake,
Within the mirroring water's wake.

Like patch work quilts, the trees spread color
Over grasses, shaded brown.
Spent farmlands rested in the sun.
Dame Nature's gown
Revealed each pleat of harrowed ground.

To me, she looked her loveliest!
I like October's gown the best.
The sun made diamonds on the lake,
A wedding band
From Nature's hand, held still, upon her lap of land.

I applauded the beauty of Nature and sky
And enjoyed every moment that she and I
Shared in rare tranquility.
Though I be blind,
Yet will I see all this, in vivid memory.

That's How My Weeks Pass on By

Saturday's crazy.
Sunday's lazy.
Monday it's back to the grind.
Tuesday is rush day.
Wednesday's my wash day,
By Thursday, I'm two days behind.
But, Friday is my day,
It's pay day, it's buy day,
And that's how my weeks pass on by.
From Sunday to Sunday,
I wait for that one day
I get all the love I can buy.

I'm poor as a church-mouse,
The bank took my first house,
My wife took the banker and so,
I watch the years passin'
I'm hungry, not fastin'
'Til Friday, the best day I know.

Bird Black and Sly Cat

Bird Black sat on a limb in the top
of the Live Oak tree
Where he chirped and squawked bird-talk
to his family.
He didn't believe in wasting that special
part of the day,
When the air was fresh and the sun
started on its way.
From East to West around his world
in the Live Oak tree,
Where he chirped and squawked bird-talk
to his family.

Up and down, Bird Black flew 'round the
limbs of the Live Oak tree,
Catching worms and fetching seeds and
squawking noisily.
Big sly Cat, pretending to nap, lay
stretched out flat
In the shade, on the grass near the trunk
of the Live Oak tree.
I watched the pair from my rocking chair,
which happens to be
My favorite place, on the porch of our house
near the Live Oak tree.

Big Sly Cat watched Bird Black, still
pretending not to see.
From the tree, Bird Black could see Sly Cat
and eyed him, cautiously!
I saw Bird Black and I saw Sly Cat and I know
they both saw me.

"Bird Black and Sly Cat" continues . . .

I doubted that Sly Cat was napping, but I
would wait and see.

How well I knew, Bird Black knew too, that
Cats are quick and clever.
He must watch Sly Cat, Bird Black knew that!
He could trust a cat? Not ever!

Then all at once, with one great pounce,
Sly Cat woke suddenly!
Without delay, Bird Black flew away up high
In the Live Oak tree!
It isn't right to cause such fright!
All Bird Black wants is peace,
But—Sly Cat wants a piece of bird!
Yet, I love both and each.
Poor cat! Poor bird! It's quite absurd
that both should be disturbed.
Though Nature made them enemies,
I love both cat and bird.

Bird Black is just a friendly Grackle
Who crackles constantly.
Even so, I'd miss him if he left
My Live Oak tree.
Sly Cat is just a kitten, grown,
Who purrs and paws at me.
I found him in our meadow.
He has no friends, 'cept me.
I truly would be lonely, without
dear bird and cat.
But—Nature made them enemies,
and that , I guess, is that.

The two will never get along, as much

"Bird Black and Sly Cat" continues . . .

As I might scold!
Birds and cats cannot be friends,
at least, that's what I'm told.
I have a plan that just might work!
I think it's worth a try!
I'll feed my cat until he's fat and
When Bird Black flies by,
Sly Cat will be too slow, and so,
Though friends they'll never be,
Bird Black can stay and squawk all day,
Safe, in my Live Oak tree.

Escape

How delicious could be
The act of reminiscing,
As called upon to flavor
Quiet nights
When happiness is touching,
Ever slight.
So to reach and so to find
A proper peaceful state of mind,
To enrich and so impart
A taste of bliss
To this starved heart,
Succeeding for a time,
'Til acid drops of dill and brine
Filter from the deep dark wells
Of the many private hells
That are ever part of me.

I hold too many memories
Not welcome at recall.
No matter how selective
I may be, to choose the one
That certain pleases me,
Stifled passions
Purposely confined,
Long imprisoned in the archives
Of my mind,
Escape from time to time to prick
And once more stab
The cicatrix,
Renewing wounds
That never seem to heal.
The pain returns.

"Escape" continues . . .

Instead of happiness, I find
Gross infection in my mind.
Let reason abdicate
And fate evaporate!
So, to have no memories at all,
To disconnect the heart and mind,
I shall lock my memory,
And throw the key
With all my strength
From my uncharted Limbo
Deep into the sea.

Adolescence

In early childhood, we love to pretend.
Pretense abandoned is childhood's end.
Adult modes of conduct are strictly defined.
Who wants to grow up in a world so unkind?

Often, when felled by the cruel fist of Fate,
For a while, I'll allow my mind to *swing free*,
To escape all regrets, to ignore, to forget,
To soften the blows of reality.

These moods are like fluffy white clouds
That envelope my mind and engulf my soul.
From nowhere to nowhere, they pass as they come,
When dissolved by distraction or self-control.

This mode of escape is quite risky, I'm told.
"Moods must be banished, emotions controlled."
"Keeping in step requires reason to rule,"
But life is oppressive and people are cruel.

I am tempted at times, to deliberately
Swing free from my problem, indefinitely.
I could and I would were there something to gain,
But ignoring the truth doesn't lessen the pain.

After I rest in my mental retreat,
I return a bit wiser from each defeat.
Someday, the world will accept me as me.
Then, I won't have to pretend or *swing free*.

I'll be sure of myself. I'll prove I can make it.
I'll be self-sufficient; I won't have to fake it.
Just for now, understand that I've got to *swing free*!
I don't want to grow up 'til I learn to be me.

John 13:34

She walks slowly
  through the days that yet remain,
Surviving each,
  despite such constant pain
As plagues the lonely heart
  long left behind
By the love that haunts
  the chambers of her mind.

Though dowager hump and dewlap
  betray her years,
Her wit is quick.
  Her mind is tuned and clear.
There is a vault
  of wisdom and compassion in her eyes.
Her speech is quite precise,
  never crude and ever wise.

Uncertainly, with hope,
  she seeks some confirming sign
That this postscript to her life
  has a purpose and design.
She is anxious to be helpful,
  to be needed in some way,
That so involved,
  she may find a meaning for each day.

Once, though many years ago,
  in happiness she knew
Sweet tender moments filled with love,
  as mothers do
When yawning babies'

"John 13:34" continues . . .

sleepy lips do soft express
"I love you, Mommy, good night,
and God bless."

Parents don't forget to love.
children often seem to,
Or at least give that impression,
but don't mean to,
Perhaps because they struggle
with contemporary themes
And gird for battle daily,
to realize their dreams.

Counterpoised
between self-confidence and cower,
They are out flanked
by those who flaunt inherent power.
Wounded by corruption's smite,
pricked by greed,
And ever torn between two monsters,
want and Need.

In turn and time,
we all resign to the command of age.
With tactics outdated,
we will but watch the conflict rage.
Perhaps our children's attitude
is not as it appears.
Perhaps they are completely drained,
not deaf to midnight tears.

Perhaps they need reminding,
in a very gentle way,
That example teaches well,
and that their children will repay

"John 13:34" continues . . .

The tenderness and love that they extend,
  in due respect.
Child and parent set the standards
  for the life each can expect.

Living without purpose
  is like breathing without air.
Devoid of love,
  existence will be swallowed by despair.
Each generation owes to love,
  and with love must repay.
". . . love ye one another. . ."
  he commands. We must obey.

Walk beside her
  through the days that yet remain.
Give her joy
  in love and purpose, once again,
Until she rests
  at last beyond all earthly harm.
Turn then, and gratefully accept
  your own child's loving arm.

Let's Play Bridge

"Hello. Ann? Glad you're at home!
Glad you weren't on the phone!
Is your husband still at home?"

"Put away your mop and broom.
Let's play bridge this afternoon.
We can play four rounds by noon!

"I just talked to Mary Ann.
She says she shouldn't, but she can.
She'll just throw supper in a pan."

"You know Marilyne will play.
She'd play bridge most any day.
I'll tell her that we're on our way."

"What? You put your clothes to soakin'
And found your water line was broken-
But you'll play! You must be joking!"

Called the service-man you say?
Play there? Yes, you bet! O.K.!
I'll call the girls. We're on our way."

"Hello. Marilyne? Are you free?
How 'bout some bridge with Ann and me
And Mary Ann? We'll quit at three.

"What's that? You played last night 'til three?
How bad can your headache be?
Two aspirin didn't work? Take three."

"Let's Play Bridge" continues . . .

"Harry can eat lunch alone.
Leave a message by your phone.
'You'll be at Ann's. She can't leave home'"

"Mary Ann? Hello. We'll play at Ann's
She's waiting for a service man.
Bring some lunch-meat if you can."

Six no trump, and I'm in trouble!
Should have known that Ann would double.
Tsk! Tsk! The bid's redoubled.

Why am I caught each time I fake it?
I don't know how my partner takes it.
Lord knows, I'll never make it!

Why do I love this game called "Bridge"?

My Epitaph

Here lies a non-notable
Who said nothing quotable,
Did nothing memorable,
Leaves nothing valuable,
Was literarily unacceptable
And totally unexceptional.

From dust to nothing
And back to dust.

The Class of '23

Gaily came and sadly went
Our friends of younger days,
As we met at Class Reunions
And revived our yesterdays.

We wrote letters to each other
To insure that we'd be found
When they issued invitations
As the next one rolled around.

At our Thirty-Year Reunion
We numbered twenty-five.
Some we'd lost, and had not heard
If they were still alive.

At each affair, the gift of friendship,
Which we thought was free of cost,
Took its price in sadness
Over each dear friend we'd lost.

Then, it hardly mattered
As to who did what or where.
The only things worth noting
Were the memories we shared.

At our previous reunion,
We had dwindled to just five;
Still, we planned the next affair
For those who might survive.

We spoke sadly of that someday
When, perhaps, someone would come

"The Class of '23" continues . . .

To find the Class of '23
All gone—except one.

Gaily came and sadly went
The Class of '23
Dim the lights and close the book
No one has come—but me.

Dream or Prophecy

I saw chaos and destruction
Followed by a day that never came
To anyone. I saw the sun
In familiar skies
Obediently rise
On an innocent day.

Subtle breezes searched in vain
For someone to touch,
And, not finding such,
Sighed and wistfully
Stroked the tassels
Of unharvested grain.

From space, weather satellites
Signaled, day and night,
Unheeded. Not needed.
No one will see the winter's snow,
And if the fruit trees bear in Spring,
No one will know.

I saw a city's great Cathedral
With charred doors ajar,
Inviting all to come and pray;
The time for that was yesterday.
There is no time today.

I saw empty cradles rock
To silent lullabies.
I did not know, but could surmise
The cause of this calamity:
Some insane executioner
Had silenced humanity.

"Dream or Prophecy" continues . . .

Suddenly I woke to find
The world as it had been
Before I slept.
Gratefully, I said a prayer,
Cursed that awful scare,
And quietly wept.

This dream has re-occurred since then,
the same each time, and time again.
Now I wonder constantly,
"Is this dream or prophecy?"
Could this morbid nightmare be
A preview of reality?

Parturition

Find the children! Close the doors!
I can hear the water hissing!
Search the carriage for the baby!
Missing!

Bent, tall women wearing white,
Masked below one eye of light,
Rushed about like shadows
In and out of focus.
They spoke in echoed sounds of dread,
Eye to eye and head to head,
And each concurred by turn, "She's dead."

A gushing swelled within my head.
"The children must be found" I said.
"Can't you hear the water's roar?"
"Save the children, nothing more!"
The women shook their faceless heads
From side to side, then fled from sight
Into the distance of night.

"Mad! I'm going mad!" I cried.
"Or am I dreaming? Have I died?"
These strange surroundings seem so real
And there's a numbness that I feel.

"Go back, my loved ones!
Stay away! If this is death
You must not stay!
For I am lost unless I plead
'Don't take me yet, there is a need
To save the children lest they drown!'"
There's water gushing all around!

by Joan Tenner

I am deserted, still I seek
The baby that is missing,
And the water rises, hissing.
Swelling, swirling through my head!
Chaotic lights perplex my brain.
Strange surroundings once again, and fright!
I am fearful of the night!

Broken glass in squares and pieces-
The baby blanket shows sharp creases-
But no baby wrapped inside.
"Where is my baby, Lord?" I cried.

Then—sudden peace.
Past the distances of night,
Delivered from delirium,
Devoid of flood or fright,
My baby, in soft blankets bound,
Lay sleeping, safe, beside me
In this hallowed ground.

Away—detached—
I felt aloof,
Like calm above the storm.
We were safe and kindly warm!
Beyond the bonds of earth are we,
My darling baby-child and me,
Together for eternity.

Summer

It's so easy to write poems
About Winter, Fall and Spring
But when it comes to Summer,
I can't write one pleasant thing,

I find Summer's heat oppressive.
It's so hard to be expressive
When you're tired and hot and sweaty
And your hair hangs like spaghetti
Drooping messily about,
And the kinds run in and out
And they never shut the door!

Every game we have is played,
But somehow, never put away.
Every neighbor's kid and dog
Comes to our back yard to play,
While their own yard's trim and green,
Ours is bare and never clean,
Full of balls and bikes and dolls.

Not a moment is serene
And the house is never clean
And the yard is full of weeds
And the garden's goin' to seed
And there are weevils in the flour
And the dish cloth's always sour
And the beds are seldom made.

My neighbor called today.
The kids picked all her flowers.
I was lectured for two hours

"Summer" continues . . .

On the art of discipline,
While the kids ran out and in.
She can spend time on the phone,
With no children of her own!

Today the Minister came by.
You couldn't guess the reason why!
Its seems he needed something done.
He was looking for someone
Who could run the church bazaar,
And would my son play his guitar
At the services next Sunday?

Once the kids go back to school,
Once the days are calm and cool,
I'll have time to write again.
I can hardly wait 'til then!
In the meantime, life goes on
And the kids go out and in
And they never shut the door!

Now That I Have Time

Now that I have time,
The years ahead without design,
Now that I've accomplished the ordinary,
Learned perception and patience,
And resigned my own passions
To the enigmas of my heart,
(More restrained—though less confined)
I desire to impart what I have learned
To those who might profit in some way
From what I have to say.

Now that I have the time,
What is there left (unsaid) to say?
The feathers of last year's birds
Do not suffice for this year's nest;
Nor does the same wind blow
The same snow over the mountain crest.
Season and subject being the same—
Yet not the same (except in name),
Their time and events will not come again.

Young shoulders cannot carry the aged head.
The cautious and suspicious mind
Might stifle the joys of adventures instead
Of preventing a possible failure ahead.
Though well intended I may be,
Seeing, perhaps, all there is to see
In my own time and circumstance,
Like to another plane,
Nothing is ever the same.

"Now That I Have Time" continues . . .

All possible dimensions,
Physical, spiritual and mental,
Act, react and interact
With such variety that,
Though history is said to repeat,
The audience sits in different seats
With a different point of view.
Thus, the drama of each new moment,
At that moment, is new.

Now that I have time
To think, to advise and to write,
I recognize that I haven't the right
To pass a judgement on wrong and right,
As nothing is ever exactly the same.
Strange! I never thought about it
Quite that way, until today.
Now that I have the time,
I find that I have nothing to say.

Joan Tenner

oan Tenner began to write at an early age and continue throughout her ife. Joan's poetry became her voice that expressed her ideas, her im-pressions and her reflections of her world beyond her kitchen window s she washed the dishes, cleaned her house and cared for her children.

nspired by Henry Wadsworth Longfellow who wanted to read some simple heartfelt lay to soothe restless feelings . . . read from some umbler poet." So, Joan considered her poems as quite ordinary and imple writings;

She became that "Humble Poet!"

he has authored two volumes of poetry . . . This her first book Con-ider the Humbler Poet and a second book entitled Journey Through histles and Time. A third in the series will be available in 2024 from Visdom House Books entitled A Collection from the Humbler Poet.

Joan's Halloween stories, entitled Grandma's Halloween Stories were written between 1989 through 1996 for her grandchildren and were published by Wisdom House Books in 2020.

All her books are available at www.thehumblerpoet.com

www.ingramcontent.com/pod-product-compliance
Lightning Source LLC
Chambersburg PA
CBHW030335310726
48979CB00001B/40

* 9 7 8 1 7 3 3 2 4 4 4 6 6 *